# 2017
# GRAND PRIX
# guide

## SNIFF PETROL

# 2017 Grand Prix Guide by Sniff Petrol

Published by Sniff Petrol Limited.
sniffpetrol.com

# INTRODUCTION

Hello and welcome to the all-new 2017 Sniff Petrol Grand Prix Guide. In here you will find a handy and factually incorrect run down of all the circuits on this year's calendar, a concise and informationally dubious rundown of each team and driver, and a range of exciting features about the future of the sport, the drivers we've said goodbye to, and guest columns from stars such as Nico Rosberg and Ron Dennis, all of which contain little-to-no reliable intelligence whatsoever. But don't worry. Where once this would have been known as 'useless fictional drivel', Donald Trump has taught us it's now called 'alternative facts'. So come on, let's grab this F1 season by the Pirelli.

Sniff Petrol

# THE CHANGES FOR 2017

Fernando Alonso once said that modern F1 cars are too easy to drive, although in fairness he was talking about the 2015 McLaren and its habit of giving drivers time off after about lap 17. Even so, Formula 1 is bringing in a load of rule changes for 2017, all designed to make the cars faster and more challenging. Here are the main ways in which the FIA is probably cocking things up as usual.

### Wider tyres
Tyre width goes up by 20 centimetres, raising mechanical grip levels, increasing cornering speeds and leading to a rash of eBay adverts that start, 'tyre warmers for sale, lightly used, wrong size'. Unclear if this will be good for racing, although it's certainly good news for rubber suppliers and osteopaths who specialise in F1 pit crews.

### Increased minimum weight and fuel allowances
Fuel up by five kilos, overall weight up by 20 kilos, the latter being good news for Lewis Hamilton who can drive without removing most of his piercings.

### Extended noses
All teams are permitted to give their cars much larger noses this season in a process known technically as 'Prosting'. The 20cm increase allows for bigger front wings, giving greater downforce and more opportunity for one of the shit drivers to run over his own teammate's nose at the first corner.

### Bargeboards
The massive side attachments are back, with the twin aims of managing aero and giving the drivers something to bang their knee on as they get in. One of the reasons Nico Rosberg has left F1 is because he was completely incapable of exiting the

car gracefully as it was, and he wanted out before he got snared in the web of his own side panels like a heavily branded fly.

## New rear wings

For 2017 the rear wings get lower and wider and also more slanted for some reason, and they sit further rearwards on the car. Downforce increases, as does the resemblance to one of those cool F1 cars from the 1980s, so it's yin and yang really. Or shit and not shit. Unfortunately, as a result of the lower wing most entries have a massive fin on top because the FIA forgot to ask the teams not to make their cars look like shit sharks.

## Rear diffuser

The diffuser, like the wing above it, gets bigger and more downforcey for 2017, although unlike the wing above it, the diffuser is unlikely to be plastered in adverts for shitty horrible drinks and a type of condom only sold in Madagascar.

## Summary

For some time the people in charge of Formula 1 have realised that the cars have too much grip on fresh tyres to look exciting and generate too much downforce to permit close racing. That's why for 2017 they have altered the rules to increase tyre grip and downforce to a huge degree, thereby... OH FOR FUCK'S SAKE, NOT AGAIN.

# TEAM PROFILE - MERCEDES

**Full name:** Mercedes AMG Petronas Motorsport
**Car:** W08 Hybrid
**Engine:** Mercedes
**Drivers:** Lewis Hamilton, Valtteri Bottas

The reigning world champions must be the team to beat this season unless they do something really stupid like fit a Honda engine. Behind the scenes there have been changes for 2017 with the departure of Paddy Lowe, which is fine because he was basically the spare boss and it was never quite clear what he did anyway, a position known in motorsport as 'The Sam Michael'. There are changes in the car too since Nico Rosberg realised he had a horrible pain in his arse and could only get rid of it by ceasing to work with Lewis Hamilton. Speaking of which, Hamilton remains a supreme talent and blessed with an effortless ability in all conditions to really irritate people. The formerly British driver and his strangely peripatetic accent, now free of having to race alongside a friend he completely hated, is totally focussed on winning a fourth world championship and has been spending up to seven hours a day in the gym, posing next to the equipment for Instagram photos. With Nico Rosberg stepping down to spend more time with his lack of enthusiasm for F1, stern Finnish man-baby Valtierri Bottas occupies the vacant seat bringing with him a quietly understated level of skill, experience and ability not to lose his shit when Hamilton is inevitably some sort of dick to him.

# TRACK GUIDE - AUSTRALIA

**Track:** Melbourne Grand Prix Circuit
**Race date:** 26 March

The season kicks off in its traditional Australian home, at a circuit that demands high downforce on account of being upside down. Albert Park is always popular with fans thanks to its pleasant, city centre location and expansive views, offering plenty of chances to watch the racing while relaxing with a fresh shoe full of Champagne. The home crowd will of course be rooting for local boy Daniel Ricciardo, although by the time they get there Lewis Hamilton might also have developed an Australian accent too. Expect plenty of action, largely from F1 journalists having to file reports about how it was/wasn't like that in testing.

## AUSTRAL-O-FACTS
- Local bylaws mean each pit garage must contain at least one barbecue.
- Chances of poisonous spider attack – high
- The national symbol of Australia is currently in London working in a gym.
- Melbourne is known as the cultural capital of Australia because it used to have a library.

# TRACK GUIDE - CHINA

**Track:** Shanghai International Circuit
**Race date:** 9 April

One of the modern meh tracks, the Shanghai venue known as 'that one with the things above the pit straight' has been on the calendar for years, although for some reason it doesn't feel like it. The Tilke-designed track delivers low brake wear and charisma, but scores highly for number of corners and quantity of empty grandstands with covers on them to make it seem as if they're supposed to be like that. In recent years, Chinese authorities were controversially planning to waive the requirement for competitors to wear a head and neck restraint, though experts warned the drivers against it, hence the popular motorsport expression, 'Don't push too hard your dreams for China to bin your HANS'.

## CHIN-O-FACTS
- The most popular type of takeaway meal in China is Chinese.
- People in China are not very interested in motorsport, unless the government instructs them otherwise.
- The Great Wall of China is the only piece of factually incorrect trivia visible from space.

# A HEARTY HOWDY FROM CHASE CAREY

Howdy sports fans. It's your new buddy Chase Carey here to tell you that I'm real excited to be assumin' control of this here Formulation 1 sport. Now y'all might be wondering why I haven't taken over things a little sooner and the truth is that we had ourselves a good ol' fashioned vermin problem at the headquarters. But don't you worry cuz we dealt with the little varmint by making him emeritus chairman.

So you might wondering what old Chase here is going to do with the Formulised 1. Well folks, I don't believe in rushing things so for the time being everything is gonna stay juuuus' the way it is, at least until your friend Chase here can get his noggin' around all these new rules. It sure is a head scratcher!

Anyways, the Big CC is sure looking fo ___ ___ to sippin' a cool sarsaparilla and watching som automobile racing around the world and n all the guys at the teams. Wow, they su names, like Maclarryin and Force It I and I sure do admire their matching ! But boy, do those guys drive fast! W Louise Hamiltown might do over 15

Moceedes. If you tried that on the road instead of on one of these fancy race tracks like Moanser, Silverstones or Subangbang gosh dang I reckon the cops would lock you away!

Course, there's gonna come a time when yours truly here might want to start making some adjustments to the old Formalised 1 and I hope y'all won't mind that. It sure is a mighty fine sport you got here, but maybe I'll have to ask if some of this stuff is really necessary. I mean, I'm a broad minded kind of guy, but I wonder if it's really suitable for families to watch a sport in which every car has a curse system on board. Sheesh, if the driving guy wants to say a profane word, let him do it himself, as long as there are no children around of course. Also, there sure is a lot of travelling and some of it seems to be to places where they don't give a rat's behind about the Formutation 1, and that's a little strange. Oh, hey, total change of subject but does anyone know why there's a bunch of discarded brown envelopes with foreign writing on them behind the radiator in my new office? Where was I? Oh yes, making some changes. Another thing I might take a look-see at is those driving guys. They sure is funny! I like the way they say 'for sure' but they don't seem 'for sure' 'bout anything, 'cept maybe that the 'guys did a good job'. And I admire that 'cuz, as I always say, there ain't no 'I' in 'tediously repetitive'!

Speaking of teams, y'all know I can't run this here Formicatable 1 all on my ownsome. I'd have to be a crazy midget full of monkey serum to try that! That's why I'm super delighted to welcome my special deputy Roscoe P. Brawn who's gonna talk to all the team guys and see if we can't just fix up the tire rotations and DREnd Zones and such like so that maybe, jus' maybe, it's all a little more interesting. But hey, adda I know?

In the meantimes, I look forward to travelling all over to a series of largely identical race tracks that allow ter action where I can spend my time trying to gosh darn incredibly and needlessly complex regulations. Maybe then old Chase here can start to figure out why in darnation people aren't interested in this sport! Y'all take care now. And next time, come out from behind that grey bush when I'm talkin' to y'all. Oh wait, darnit, that's my moustache!

## TEAM PROFILE - RED BULL

**Full name:** Red Bull Racing
**Car:** RB13
**Engine:** TAG Heuer oh God are we going through this again
**Drivers:** Daniel Ricciardo, Max Verstappen

Red Bull gave it their best shot to topple Mercedes in 2016 and might have done it if only they weren't running a Renault engine with 'Renault' crossed out and 'TAG Heuer' written on in marker pen. Unfortunately for them, the same is true this year, although Renault have promised more power, more efficiency and an attractive zero percent finance offer (on Le Bop special edition models only). The new RB13 is being billed by the team with the ballsy tagline 'unlucky for some', a slogan Daniil Kvyat is doing his best not to take personally. It's an interesting design of car, showing all the hallmarks of smooth headed human computer Adrian Newey, especially in the unusual design of the nose. Red Bull is still awaiting confirmation from the FIA that it's within the spirit of the rules if, during a race, the car harvests ants as fuel. Last year, the supreme talents of both drivers allowed the sometimes sluggish car to punch above its weight and the successful pairing of a human smile with an insolent teenager remains the same for 2017. Daniel Ricciardo has spent the off season developing a new schtick to follow on from his shoe drinking shenanigans and now intends to celebrate every podium place by eating some cake out of his own underpants. Meanwhile, surly youth Max Verstappen promises to be less distracted by outside factors, especially as one of his GCSEs is photography and it's mostly coursework based.

# TRACK GUIDE – BAHRAIN

**Track:** Bahrain International Circuit
**Race date:** 16 April

Now a fixture on the F1 calendar, Bahrain is a high speed track that's tough on engines and brakes with long straights followed by tight corners such as the run up to Imprisoned Dissenters straight into Incarcerated Homosexuals bend, or the sprint down Confiscated Passport and on into the tricky Forced Labour complex. This track is popular with drivers who like high speed, and not popular with Kimi Raikkonen because he can't get a drink and he's convinced he keeps being introduced to ghosts. Hazards at this track include heat, dust, and the risk of Jackie Stewart mistaking you for a member of the local royal family and then attempting to have a toadying conversation with you for 40 minutes.

## BAHRAIN-O-FACTS
- Bahrain's main industries are dust, torture and dusty torture.
- Bahrain is prone to strong winds, in particular the summertime Shamal which is unpleasant, unreliable and has a horrible clock.
- Bahrain has been criticised for its human rights abuses, though Bernie Ecclestone ignored concerns about cruelty, mental torture and financial punishment, and since he's no longer running F1 he won't be able to do those things any more.
- Women's rights in Bahrain took a major step forward in 2008 when the government asked men to pick a day of the week on which they beat their wives more gently.
- Bahrain has a thriving tourism industry as every year people flock to see attractions such as the very dusty table. It's very dusty.

# TRACK GUIDE - RUSSIA

**Track:** Sochi Autodrom
**Race date:** 30 April

One of the longest tracks on the calendar, Sochi is ideal for anyone who enjoys seeing cars driving in a procession around a drab industrial estate that seems to have been photo bombed by Rolex ads. There are plenty of fast sections including the Putin Is Great straight, the Glorious Putin Is A Very Manly Man Person bend, and of course Putin Is Not A Weasel Faced Nutjob curve. Drivers who say they enjoy this track are all the ones who want to see their families alive again. With micro commander Bernard Ecclestone off the scene, it will be interesting to see if Vladimir Putin makes his traditional appearance at the race in the country he rules. We'll have to wait until 22 October to find out.

## RUSS-O-FACTS
- In terms of area, Russia is what geographers call 'fucking massive'.
- Russia has a thriving political debating culture which is generally divided into two sides – people who support Vladimir Putin and people who go missing.
- Russia recently passed a bill decriminalising domestic violence, a move that was condemned by the rest of the world, apart from Adrian Sutil.
- Russian president Vladimir Putin is a big fan of riding a horse with no shirt on, being completely heterosexual and not supressing anything, no siree.

# TEAM PROFILE - FERRARI

**Full name:** Scuderia Ferrari
**Car:** SF7 OH!
**Engine:** Ferrari
**Drivers:** Sebastian Vettel, Kimi Raikkonen

There was embarrassment for Ferrari before testing as the automated system that puts out their two annual statements accidentally released the one that says 'We don't like these proposals and we're thinking of leaving' which is supposed to come toward the end of the season, rather than the correct one for this time of year which says, 'We think this could be our year to win the Championship'. The new SF7 OH! has looked promising in early testing, which is a surprise since they has clearly looked at every available aero option and decided to use all of them at once. This might be because the team has now sorted out its wind tunnel after finding a settings menu it previously thought was just for adjusting the backlight. In the face of new rules, the team has opted for stability in its ranks, keeping scrap metal dealer turned team principal Maurizio Arrivabuses as boss, though he's been in the job for over two years and is surely due to be sacked soon. The drivers also remain as last season, with Sebastian Vettel shouldering off-track tasks such as shaking hands with sponsors and forming complete sentences, whilst maintaining his new on-track role of getting exasperated with younger drivers like your dad tutting at bad manoeuvring at the local tip. Alongside Vettel is Raikkonen who is going to keep looking like a man who is tolerating this party because he knows he's going to sneak off to a better party later.

# TRACK GUIDE - SPAIN

**Track:** Circuit de Barcelona-Catalunya
**Race date:** 14 May

The Barcelona track is a great one for fans, offering a wonderful climate and excellent views from all seats making it the perfect place from which to observe a joyless procession for 90 minutes. This is of course the home race of Fernando Alonso which means at least he can get out and go to see his family when the McLaren goes wrong. Catalunya is almost unique in the F1 calendar for combining a long straight with many fast and slow corners, and yet managing to be so boring that you actually feel the life draining from your body at around lap 19. The track is well-known to all drivers because it is used extensively in testing, although not to Kimi Raikkonen because he wasn't paying attention.

## SPAN-O-FACTS
- Barcelona is not in Spain, it's in Catalunya, which is in Spain.
- Barcelona is home to the famous Sagrada Familia, one of the world's most breathtaking displays of scaffolding.
- Spain suffered an oppressive system until 1975 when the death of General Franco allowed SEAT to stop basing all its cars on old Fiats.
- Southern Spain is famed for containing the world's largest and most thriving colony of retired British racists.

# TRACK GUIDE - MONACO

**Track:** Circuit de Monaco
**Race date:** 28 May

For many the jewel in the crown of the F1 calendar, Monaco is a glittering, glamorous event that allows Europe's most leathery people the opportunity to stand around pretending to be interested in motorsport. For actual fans, Monaco presents the chance to spend a massive amount of money getting horribly sunburnt or miserably drenched while watching no overtaking whatsoever, truly making it the quintessence of Formula 1. For drivers, Monaco is a tight, technical, challenging track and one which is unique in giving them the chance to shout, 'Hey, you can see my house from here'. For everyone involved in F1, few tracks are as evocative as Monaco, bringing a tingle to the spine with the mere mention of illustrious corners such as Sainte-Devote, Mirabeau and La Rascasse, as well as lesser known complexes such as Russian Hooker, Tax Dodge and Horrible Sunglasses.

## MONAC-O-FACTS
- The correct name for a person from Monaco is a Mongoose.
- Nico Rosberg spent over $1m renovating his Monaco home to get it exactly as he wanted it, and then immediately sold it.
- The noise and bustle of the Monaco GP makes the ideal time to make a run for it, if you're stuck in a loveless marriage to a royal.
- In order to enjoy full tax exempt status in Monaco, residents must regularly submit utility bills and evidence that they own at least 750 kilos of gold jewellery.

# TEAM PROFILE - FORCE INDIA

**Full name:** Sahara Force India F1 Team
**Car:** VJM10
**Engine:** Mercedes
**Drivers:** Sergio Perez, Esteban Ocon

The current kings of the top mid-field, Force India had a strong 2016 in which they rarely did anything as attention seeking as get on the podium but quietly trucked along, racking up enough points to finish fourth in the constructors' championship, to the surprise of everyone including themselves. They'll be looking to repeat that almost completely unnoticeable excellence, but their 2017 won't be without problems. Cyril Abiteboul recently singled out Force India as the type of less-well-funded team that will suffer in the F1 'arms race', momentarily forgetting that he is the boss of the yellow and black shit shower that is Renault. However, it is true that this is not the most cash rich of teams and the car is not the best looking either, with its soggy proboscis and a stepped nose like that bit everyone trips over in the hallway of a cheap rented flat. Also in the cause-for-concern file, team owner Vijay Mallya appears to be turning into a Las Vegas magician. On the plus side, the Merc engines should be strong, driving regular Sergio Perez is prone to moments of goodness, and Manor escapee Esteban Ocon is tipped for great things, plus he's French so he can get flick knives and untipped cigarettes which he can sell to the other kids at school.

# TRACK GUIDE - CANADA

**Track:** Circuit Gilles Villeneuve
**Race date:** 11 June

The much-loved Canadian Grand Prix takes place in its traditional home of Circuit Gilles Villeneuve, aside from that one disastrous year when they tried to run it at the Circuit Jacques Villeneuve, only to find everything was just baggy and annoying and kept playing shit-awful guitar music. Also, the top section was thinning and trying to pretend it wasn't. Canada is one of the shorter circuits on the calendar but also one of the toughest with plenty of chances to smack into a wall. That's particularly true of the infamous final corner with its legendary hazard, often wrongly referred to as 'the wall of champions' but actually known locally as 'the wall of champignons' because it is entirely made of mushrooms. Drivers to have come a cropper on this hazard include Sebastian Vettel, Jenson Button and Pastor Maldonado, who managed to hit it even though he was competing in the Mexican Grand Prix at the time. Canada punishes engines and brakes, but being Canada it then puts them into a rehabilitation programme and makes sure they're okay.

## CANAD-O-FACTS
- Based on GDP per capita, Canada is the 20th richest nation on earth. However, based on pleasantness it is number one.
- The official language of Montreal is a sort of made-up version of French, created largely to annoy English speakers.
- Canada has some of the most stringent laws in the world. For example, being caught in possession of hard drugs is punishable by up to five years of being asked if you're okay.
- In Canada, maple syrup is a shampoo, shower gel and deodorant. That's why most Canadians are covered in bees.
- Canada has more guns per person than the USA yet somehow manages not to behave like a total dick with them.

# TRACK GUIDE - AZERBAIJAN

**Track:** Baku City Circuit
**Race date:** 25 June

For 2017 the Baku race loses its title of Grand Prix of Europe and gains the more realistic title, Grand Prix of the Outer Moons of Fucking Saturn. When Azerbaijan decided it needed a Grand Prix, they wanted a street circuit that was radical and exciting. Unfortunately, Hermann Tilke has got some shit-hot search engine optimisation going on, and they ended up hiring him. Baku is fast for a street circuit because it's long and has some sizeable straights, offset by slow corners, and also the vast number of stray horses that roam the city centre, praying on local sugar lump vendors and making life for its residents a turdy misery. Drivers must also remember to look out for that bit where some idiot has built a 12th century tower on the track.

## AZERBAIJAN-O-FACTS

- A recent survey showed that 87 percent of people do not know where Azerbaijan is. This is particularly the case in Northern Europe, America, and Azerbaijan.
- Azerbaijan makes a great deal of money from oil, but its other exports include phlegm, shouting, and funny cat videos.
- The country has a very poor human rights record, according to a study by that Baku university department where all the academics mysteriously disappeared.
- Due to a terrible mix-up, all Azerbaijanian money carries a picture of Joe Pesci.
- One F1 person who doesn't like going to Azerbaijan is Nico Hulkenberg as he resembles the logo for the country's leading brand of lavatory cleaner. 'It's very difficult,' he explains. 'Everywhere I go, people shout at me, "under the rim!" I get enough of that in Germany.'

## NICO ROSBERG WRITES…

Hi guys. Yea, for sure it's Nico Rosberg here! You know, a lot of people were surprised when I announced my retirement from Formula 1 and for sure those people included me. You know, a lot of guys said to me, but Nico, you were just F1 world champion and for sure I replied, I know! That's why I woke up one morning, I looked at my beautiful family, and I thought wow, I have driven in the 2016 Formula 1 season and become the 2016 Formula 1 world champion and, wow, I'm not doing that again, it was horrible! Also, I have just totally got into *Cash In The Attic* and it clashes with my training schedule. Sorry guys, but something's got to give and for sure it is my career in top level motorsport.

So for sure, you guys are wondering what is next for Nico Rosberg. (That's me, by the way, my name is Nico Rosberg. Hi!) Well, I'm totally pleased to exclusively reveal to you my future plans for sure. The truth of the matter is that I am going to open a patisserie. You see, many years ago my father also owned a patisserie and I remember this distinctly from my childhood growing up in Monaco and Germany and all the other places I am from. While the other kids were out doing normal kid stuff like practising their braking points in a go-kart or working on their marketing strategies for attracting sponsorship deals, I was watching my father gently simmering another pot of confectioner's custard or selling someone a tray of petit fours. And for sure, people would say to me, 'Little Nico, maybe one day you will be a patisserer like your daddy' and I would say, 'but I don't want to run a patisserie like my daddy' but for sure no one was listening because my dad also had a very noisy car and might have been a Formula 1 driver I think.

So for sure, now is my time to devote myself to something I never really wanted to do but which everyone expected me to get involved with because of my dad and, for sure, I will put a brave face on it and run a pretty successful patisserie for a few years, although people will say it could be more successful at times, and then one day I hope to win patiserrer of the year and then at last I will retire from this total misery, for sure!

So guys, that is my plan and I hope you are able to go through the motions of pretending to like it just as much as I am! For sure, my family name is good in the patisserie business, I have the premises, all I need is someone to work in the shop alongside me but who is a total dick to me! Oh, and also a tall guy who can manage the place and will split us up when we fight, and maybe an assistant manager who has a red hat and a foul mouth. Yea guys, that sounds fantastic.

Anyway, I totally feel like this column is going great, so I'm going to unexpectedly stop.

# TEAM PROFILE - WILLIAMS

**Full name:** Williams Martini Racing
**Car:** FW40
**Engine:** Mercedes
**Drivers:** Felipe Massa (still), Lance Stroll

2017 will be interesting for Williams after a disappointing 2016 left them at the crossroads between best-of-the-rest and bit-shit-again. On the plus side, they have Merc power and the Martini livery which is scientifically proven to take off 0.5s per lap. However, this year there are a couple of problems and both of them are allowed to drive the car. Felipe Massa is somehow back in a seat he should have vacated two seasons ago, having done the equivalent of loudly breaking up with someone and then deciding to go on holiday with them. If this was the championship for being an impersonation of a scared panda, Massa would be number one but it's not so he's not. Last year this wasn't a problem because they had Bottas to bring it home in the mid-to-low points but now the second car is occupied by eyebrowsy spoilt child Lance Stroll. The newcomer's father is a Canadian fashion magnate worth $2.4 billion, which goes to show there's a surprising amount of money in denim, and while the new driver might look like he's escaped from a 1990s teen comedy movie he doesn't remember the '90s at all on account of being 12. Despite the fortune behind him, Stroll denies any advantage and insists it's perfectly normal for your dad to have replicas of all 20 tracks built on his land. For Williams 2017 is significant because they're celebrating 40 years in F1, giving a great excuse for Claire Williams to bake another yummy, yummy cake.

# TRACK GUIDE - AUSTRIA

**Track:** Red Bull Ring
**Race date:** 9 July

The [insert name of sponsor] Ring is one of the oldest tracks in F1, although it has changed much over the years after the owners discovered it was too interesting and hired Hermann Tilke to ruin it as best he could. In lap times, this is the shortest circuit on the calendar and the lap record is a staggering 52 seconds, as set by Pastor Maldonado, although that time doesn't include having to go back and apologise to all the people on the campsite. With its fast straights and intense elevations, this circuit requires the driver to make full use of the engine but not, according to Nico Rosberg last year, the steering. The Red Bull Ring is said to be the perfect match for its sister circuit, the Vodka Ring, although competing at both will lead inevitably to the Heart Palpitations Drome and the legendary Circuit du Puke In A Taxi.

## AUSTR-O-FACTS

- Austria isn't the same as Australia and it's worth knowing this when booking surprisingly cheap plane tickets.
- On that note, Mark Webber is Australian and not Austrian, and does not enjoy being followed round Homebase by someone shouting, Guten tag! Wie geht's mate!?'
- Famous Austrians in F1 include Toto Wolff and Niki Lauda, which means that 38 percent of F1 is Austrian (by height).
- To celebrate Christian Klien's time in F1 Austria has erected a statue. It is of someone else in the hope that it will distract everyone from thinking about Christian Klien's time in F1.
- The Austrian word for 'hello' is 'fuck', which is also the Austrian word for 'yes', 'what?' and 'goodbye', at least according to this phrasebook we got off Gerhard Berger.

# TRACK GUIDE - BRITAIN

**Track:** Silverstone Circuit
**Race date:** 16 July

Silverstone is one of the most famous and long-established tracks in F1 with its legendary landmarks such as Stowe, Copse and Becketts, as well as lesser-known corners such as Jackie Stewart, Sir Jackie Stewart, Three Time World Champion Jackie Stewart and Oh God, Jackie Stewart Has Got Into The Track Map Office Again. Silverstone punishes drivers who can't handle its fast corners, and fans who don't like the smell of hot onions and candy floss. With two British drivers taking part this season (pending Lewis Hamilton's real accent being found again), the mostly-in-Northamptonshire circuit is a treat for British fans who can wave a Union Flag around without looking like a dim racist. That said, Silverstone in recent years has failed to match the extraordinary spectacle of the 1980s when everyone caught Mansell Fever, a terrible disease which causes the sufferer to develop a monotonous voice and moustache.

## BRIT-O-FACTS
- Britain is the fifth richest country in the world, and the number one exporter of drizzle, swearing and describing the best thing that has ever happened to you in your entire life as 'quite good'.
- After the UK narrowly voted for Brexit, from now on all visitors will be asked to re-set their watches to 1953.
- Britain is powered by a mixture of gas, coal, nuclear and an outdated sense of its own importance.
- Great Britain is home to the English language which, like a lot of things in the country, is deliberately complicated just to annoy foreigners.

# TEAM PROFILE - McLAREN

**Full name:** McLaren Honda Formula 1 Team
**Car:** MCL32
**Engine:** Honda
**Drivers:** Fernando Alonso, Stoffel Vandoorne

An object lesson in how much attention you can get by painting something orange (see also: Donald Trump), the MCL32 is meant to mark a new start for the Woking team, based around the principle of thinking, 'What would Ron do?' and then doing the exact opposite. Hence the colour/name change and the decision to launch the car from the set of a charity telethon. All these measures have been brought about by new boss Zak Brown whose determination to be the opposite of his predecessor extends to radical measures like speaking in short sentences made up of things that are actually words. Also, apparently the factory is 'a right shithole' these days as staff are encouraged to leave the washing up, spill Vimto on the desks and participate in events such as Walk Dog Turds Into Reception Friday. Amidst all this change, Honda were asked if they fancy not being crap this season but appear to have misheard the question. Driver-wise, Alonso remains the same, though he's lost the beard that made him look like that Spanish poet who stole your girlfriend last summer, and if the car works he might also stop seeming so pissed off he's actually laughing about it. In the other car, Jenson Button has been relieved of his duties, allowing him to spend more time with his collection of supermodels, and driving chores will be handled by something called Stoffel Vandoorne, which is a type of massive cartoon cat.

# TRACK GUIDE - HUNGARY

**Track:** Hungaroring
**Race date:** 30 July

Hungary is one of the longest serving venues in F1, unless you're Martin Brundle who for several years appeared to think it wasn't happening and didn't bother to turn up. The Hungaroring provides a good mix of fast corners and slow corners, adding up to a race that's just sort of always there and might be quite good but might not be, making it very much the Force India of Grand Prix. British drivers tend to have memorable moments here, such as when Damon Hill won by 72 seconds in 1993, or when Jenson Button won from 14th in 2006, or when Johnny Herbert found a coin on the ground outside the main entrance in 2014, but then wasn't sure which country it was from and eventually just gave it to Simon Lazenby, but then couldn't stop worrying that it was really valuable and was so worried that he wasn't concentrating and walked into an airing cupboard door and broke a bit of his face.

## HUNGAR-O-FACTS

- Hungary is a country and not the same as the feeling of wanting to eat something, a fact worth remembering before accidentally buying plane tickets instead of a bag of crisps.
- Budapest is actually made up of two cities either side of the Danube with the city of Budapes on one side and the city of t on the other.
- The national booze drink of Hungary is unicum, which gives anyone drinking it a good sense of what it would be like to down a glass of burnt twigs and then fall over.

# TRACK GUIDE - BELGIUM

**Track:** Circuit de Spa-Francorchamps
**Race date:** 27 August

One of the jewels in the F1 crown, Spa is famous for having a corner that is very fast and very uphill, all at the same time. Spa is full of legendary corners such as Eau Rouge, Blanchimont and Pouhon, as well as lesser known corners such as Pamplemousse, Oiseau, and of course Jean-Jacques et Marie habite a La Rochelle. Spa is a favourite amongst drivers because it's challenging, the variable weather can level the playing field, and they all get free chips. Formula 1 is very popular in Belgium, not only because it is home to this world-class track but also thanks to the efforts of famous Belgian drivers such as Thierry Boutsen, Jacky Ickx and Lewis van der Hamilton.

## BELG-O-FACTS
- In a recent survey, 78 percent of Belgians said their favourite food was hot air balloons. It was later agreed that the wording of the survey was 'confusing'.
- Famous Belgians include the King of Belgium, the Prime Minister of Belgium and of course the person who won the X Factor in Belgium.
- Belgium was the first country in the world to legalise horses.

# MY FAVOURITE PLACES

**F1 journalist and terrible tit Trentham Sleaves picks his favourite venues on the calendar**

If you're lucky enough to go to all the F1 races in a season, as of course I am, it's natural that you'll have some favourites, though of course they're all great in different ways and I'm certainly not saying that I want to hand in the all-season paddock pass which I have and you don't! If, however, one had to pick highlights I suppose my first would be Melbourne. There's an intangible crackle in their air down under as the F1 circus re-assembles after the off season and you can almost taste it like the fine Champagne that I will almost certainly drink to welcome back our beloved sport after its winter slumbers. Cheers! For me, dear old Melby is best summed up by the weather, the laid-back location in the middle of the city and by a charming little Italian restaurant much frequented by us old hands of F1 and which discretion prevents me from naming. Only last year, I was dining alone here when I spotted my old mate Danny Ricciardo entering the place with a couple of chums. You can imagine that The Riccster (as I call him) gets a lot of attention in his Antipodean home but I was delighted when he approached my table and then quipped, 'Oh Jeez, I don't wanna sit anywhere near *that* guy' and asked to be seated elsewhere! Such a brilliant sense of humour! He ordered a mineral water that night and no, he didn't drink it from a shoe! Although he did tell the waiter 'that creepy British guy' was 'staring' and I was asked to leave! Great pranks! Sadly, as I was being bundled from the restaurant, I bumped into 'Dr' Jonathan Palmer who insisted on talking to me for a wearying 20 minutes until I claimed I had a meeting and escaped. But don't let that put you off Melbourne for it is truly the jewel of the top-level motorsport scene in south eastern Australia.

Another stop on the calendar that holds a special place in my heart is of course Monaco. Naturally, some people will complain that it's a boring procession being regarded with disinterest by the super-rich, but for me it's the very soul of F1. I love to wander the tiny streets, popping into chic cafes or dodging into an alleyway when I see Jonathan Palmer coming and then hoping he hasn't spotted me. Then there is the glamorous evening whirl of yacht parties, not open to the public of course but accessible to those of us with the right pass, which of course I have, and assuming you can find somewhere that won't tell you to 'sod off, you tedious wanker'. Oh that Eddie Jordan, such a wit! They say if you can remember the Monaco Grand Prix you probably weren't there on the Thursday evening but one of my favourite memories was several years ago when I found myself in the room of a certain well-known former world champion who was quite shocked when he emerged from the shower, demonstrated a surprising grasp of both English swear words and my neck, and no longer speaks to me except to call me a 'stalker shit'! I guess you could say, I won't be Mika invited back-inen!

A rundown of my favourite F1 venues would not be complete without the *grand dame du belle fromage* of race tracks by which of course I mean Silverstone. This is of course the 'home' race for so many of the teams, as well as my own home circuit, though of course I stay in a delightful hotel nearby, the name of which I won't share for obvious reasons, and besides you're probably one of those people who likes camping. I know some complain about the traffic and the miles of walking and the facilities, but that's because they're not an F1 journalist and don't have a media pass like me. I have too many happy memories of British Grands Prixes but one that sticks in the mind is of attending a private soiree held by a well-known team at which I was surprised to bump into a certain very well-known former world champion who had famously left this team under rather inauspicious circumstances. 'What are you doing here?' I quipped in a low voice, presuming he wouldn't want anyone to Fernand-know he was there! 'Oh my God,' he jested. 'It's you. Please, leave me alone!' Such a wonderful sense of fun! Unfortunately, I then spotted Jonathan Palmer waving enthusiastically at me from across the marquee and I had to sprint into the lavatories to hide before he insisted on talking to me!

My F1 year wouldn't be complete without Silverstone, and the same is true of another *vache sacre* (sacred cow) of the calendar, by which I mean of course Spa. If you've never been to this gem of a track, nestling deep in the Ardennes forest then don't worry because I have and it's tremendous. The racing is always a marvellous spectacle to behold from the comfort of the media area, the scenery is tremendous, and of course there is so much history to digest, perhaps accompanied by a delicious glass of crisp white wine. Enchante! I remember once dining alone the night before the race in a delightful little Italian place very near the track. Don't waste your time trying to find it as it's very much for those of us in the know. With this in mind, it was no surprise to look up from my delicious food to see a certain very well-known former team boss looming over me as he attempted to squeeze into the adjacent table. Heads were turning as it was clear that this dapper gent was, shall we say, no Flavio Bria-tourist! 'Good evening my friend,' I quipped to him in Italian, which I speak by the way. 'What?' he shot back in English. 'Oh Jesusy Chris, is this guy. Total dick man, heh? We move to other table.' And with that he was gone! Such a character! At this point my evening was compromised as Jonathan Palmer walked past, spotted me eating alone, and confronted me about my earlier claim that I couldn't go for a drink with him because I was 'busy'. That's Spa for you, I suppose! It's certainly changeable and you never know what's coming next, even if it's gobbling down the rest of your spaghetti so you can get away as quickly possible!

Finally, I cannot wrap up this reflection on F1 venues I very much enjoy going to, and being at, and standing in the paddock of because I have a pass that allows me to do that without mentioning one of the relative newcomers to the scene, by which I mean Austin, Texas, US of A. Yes, the GP o' the States has been with us only a few short years yet already it feels like an old friend with its good ol' southern hospitality and a truly unique atmosphere. I vividly remember my first time here and the warm welcome we were given to this brand-new track. I remember remarking to my old mate Martin Brundle that it was marvellous to see a new circuit make such an effort and I'll never forget what he said; 'Seriously mate, this is for Sky crew only, get out!' Always such wit and wisdom! It was at this first Austin race that I also discovered a wonderful little Italian place that has become a must-visit on my trips to the Lone Star state and which obviously I will refrain from naming. It was in here that I encountered a certain well-known 1996 world champion who exclusively revealed to me that he was going to 'get a bloody injunction if you don't leave me alone, you weirdo'. Always great to see an ex-driver Damon-strating a superb sense of humour! My affection for Austin has not diminished, even after the following year when I had to ask hotel security to clear my room of Jonathan Palmer.

Another F1 season is about to rev up and I for one cannot wait to take my front row seat for all the action. These are some of the circuits I love, but which is my favourite? Well, it would be impossible to choose because all the tracks are great although of course it would be perfectly fine for F1's new owners to get rid of whichever ones they think would be best and introduce some new ones which will also be excellent I'm sure. But, for this season at least, I can't wait to get going. Because remember, whichever track we're talking about, I will be there and you won't.

# TEAM PROFILE - TORO ROSSO

**Full name:** Scuderia Toro Rosso
**Car:** STR12
**Engine:** Renault
**Drivers:** Daniil Kvyat, Carlos Sainz

The team often known as 'spare Red Bull' is back with a more distinctive livery that manages to be very attractive, despite carrying sponsorship for a drink that taste like cornershop cola mixed with actual amphetamines. The colour scheme isn't the only thing that's changed because the team has also sold its old Ferrari engines, and been disappointed at their resale value because it didn't order them in red with cream leather interior. The second-hand Ferrari units are on eBay because this season Red Bull has decreed that Toro Rosso must suffer as they do, and insisted they run Renault engines. Conversely, Franz Tost has got tired of the big school boys stealing his stuff and has taken the precaution of having the team name stitched onto Carlos Sainz's neck. The Spanish driver continues to show great promise, particularly now he's been convinced that he doesn't need a bloke sitting next to him reading out unfathomable code about jumps and corners from a tatty sheaf of papers. With guidance from his dad, he may even one day excel at the tricky discipline of lobbing a crash helmet through the back window of a Toyota Corolla. Meanwhile, second driver Daniil Kvyat plods on, awaiting the invention of another, worse Red Bull team to which he can be demoted.

# TRACK GUIDE - ITALY

**Track:** Autodromo Nazionale Monza
**Race date:** 3 September

Monza is one of the classics, as well as one of the fastest tracks on the calendar, and is set to get even faster this year with plans to remove the Rettifilio chicane because the track's owners have sold all the speed bumps to a business park in Reading. Monza is steeped in history and it is still possible to see some parts of the old banked track, easily identified because they are covered in camera crews filming old concrete walls while facing into the sun to get a bit of lens flare for a predictable VT package to be shown just before the race. Nowhere is Monza's sense of the past better summed up than in their course cars, all of which are insanely old. Insiders say Monza's owners are set to top their own flaky achievements this year by complimenting the Ferrari 348 and mk1 Land Rover Discovery with a leggy Alfa 164 and a malfunctioning FSO Polonez.

## ITAL-O-FACTS
- In 2014 five Italian politicians were struck off for not having enough affairs.
- Italian inventions include radio, spectacles and taking your dinner order then loudly shouting something in Italian as you walk back into the kitchen so that the customer gets the uneasy sense that they are being talked about.
- Since the departure of Silvio Berlusconi, the Italian economy has suffered a 42 percent drop in bunga bunga, except in Flavio Briatore's house.

# TRACK GUIDE - SINGAPORE

**Track:** Marina Bay Street Circuit
**Race date:** 17 September

Singapore is sometimes described as the very essence of modern F1, although only in the sense that it allows extremely rich people to pay little attention to what's happening whilst standing on a yacht. The track itself winds around the city and, since Singapore is a night race, every F1 commentator is allowed to mention Blade Runner once per hour. Being a street circuit, the surface can be uneven, which gives suspension a work out, and the brakes are also tested by a track that always delights fans of medium speed corners. A fixture on the calendar since 2008, the Singapore Grand Prix is now officially the most exciting thing to happen in Singapore and once it ends all residents are required to return to their homes and sit tidily in a chair until the next year's race. For spectators, the most important thing is to not accidentally walk down the track like a big silly twat while for drivers it is vitally important not to deliberately crash, even if asked to.

## SINGAPOR-O-FACTS

- In 2004 Singapore banned chewing gum. Other things banned at the same time included wearing a white T-shirt under a black leather jacket, elbowing a jukebox so that it starts playing music, and giving a thumbs up sign while going 'Ehhhhhh'. This suite of laws was known as the Fonzarelli Act.
- Singapore is an integral part of an old British joke; 'My wife went to a terrible concert in South East Asia' 'Singapore?' 'No, it was Simply Red in Bangkok'.

# TEAM PROFILE - HAAS

**Full name:** Haas F1 Team
**Car:** VF-17
**Engine:** Ferrari
**Drivers:** Romain Grosjean, Ken Magnussen

Back for that difficult second season, it's America's only F1 team. There was no US GP, you must have dreamt it. Oh look, Bobby's getting out of the shower. Haas did surprisingly well for newbies last year, but it remains to be seen if they can repeat the trick of walking into the Ferrari parts store and asking for 'two F1 cars, please', never mind whether they can make them work again. The new car isn't the best looking thing, following a disappointing dildo 'n' fin pattern, but it's backed by a strong team working out of the proud American state of Oxfordshire. In the driving seat once again is Romain Grosjean who has defied expectation to become a surprisingly safe and skilled pair of hands now he's been taken away from the bad influence of Pastor Maldonado. The second Ferrari-branded seat with a Haas sticker over the bit that says 'Ferrari' will be taken by mild breeze Ken Magnussen who can be relied upon to avoid drawing attention to himself and in 30 years' time may look back and forget that he was ever in F1 at all. On the plus side, he is good at welding which might come in handy if the American team decides to go back to its roots for the next chassis.

# TRACK GUIDE - MALAYSIA

**Track:** Sepang International Circuit
**Race date:** 1 October

Nestling in the heart of what's known locally as 'the Sweaty Apple', Malaysia was Hermann Tilke's first big F1 track, before he'd really got his eye in on making everything completely tedious. Even so, the Sepang circuit bears many of what would become his hallmarks, being basically two massive straights with some wiggly bits in between. The track is hard on brakes and sometimes viewers, but the real challenges come from factors outside the control of a man who appears to be allergic to overtaking. The first is down to timing, and the change in light conditions during the race which is tough on drivers, particularly those who want to wear sunglasses after they've finished because it'll be dark and they'll look like pricks. The other possible challenge is the weather, specifically the potential for a massive downpour. This can be bad news for front runners who will see their lead ruined by a safety car or red flag, but good news for Kimi Raikkonen who was sort of peckish by about the fifth lap and had just remembered there was some ice cream in the freezer.

## MALAYSI-O-FACTS

- Famous Malaysians include Tony Fernandes who used to own one of the Lotuses.
- In 2007 Malaysia celebrated 50 years of independence from Britain. In 2008 it celebrated 50 years of independence from the WH Smith CD club which it didn't remember joining in the first place.
- The Malaysian currency is the ringgit, so-called because originally each coin was made up of two halves of different coins, welded together with a false serial number by a Cockney man in a workshop under a railway line.

# TRACK GUIDE - JAPAN

**Track:** Suzuka International Racing Course
**Date:** 8 October

Suzuka is one of the classic tracks on the F1 calendar, beloved by fans, enjoyed by drivers, fun to watch and amazingly not binned from the schedule for those reasons alone. For excitement, this track has it all with fast corners, slow corners, turbulent esses, and a figure-of-eight layout, although this last bit isn't that exciting unless for 2017 they've decided to delete the bridge. Suzuka is tough on engines, tough on tyres, and tough on local fans who are required to clap politely for 48 hours non-stop. The biggest random factor during the Japanese race is the weather, which could see a typhoon, in which a violent storm will lash the track, or even a typhoo, in which the entire circuit is drenched in tea.

## JAPAN-O-FACTS
- Japan is home to many car makers including Toyota, Nissan, Honda and Subaru. However, due to a horrible paper jam in the printer which everyone is too embarrassed to mend, the Japanese Car of the Year for the last 29 years has been the Isuzu Piazza.
- Japanese contains many single words for which there are no direct translations in English such as 'kujitan' which describes the feeling experienced upon leaving someone's house in a flurry of big hugs and goodbyes, then remembering you've left your jacket behind and trying to decide if you could live without the jacket for a bit because it would be too embarrassing and awkward to go back to get it.
- Japan is the world's third largest economy by GDP, and the first largest when measured by the amount spent on repairing damage caused by underwater dinosaur attacks.

# RON EXPLAINS

**Former McLaren boss Ron Dennis exclusively explains the reason why he left the team**

Verbally communicated salutational formalities, organic life forms. At this point in time, it is my expectation that you have received and processed a quantity of informations pertaining to a recent situation of circumstantial alteration regarding my employment scenario at McLaren Racing. I can confirm that this has left me in a sub-optimal situation regarding employmentitude and that a quantity of colleagues have required me to engage in a maximised quantum of desk clearification. That is to say, there has been an adjustment to the situational circumstances of my endeavours and the sudden reduction in their quantity to a reading of zero.

It seems there are persons of a high multiple who would wish from me a retrospective download of an event based nature which may furnish all those of a cerebrally curious nature an informational furnishment, thereby providing some explanitude for the reasons why I now have access to a much greater quantity of time that can be placed into the category of 'spare'. Accordingly, it brings me a measurable segment of satisfactions to furnish you with operational data regarding the situation upon which I have already discoursed, that is to say my receipt of documents being of a P45 in nature.

The datum point to which we must initially refer is that of the broad temporal spectrum referred to as November. To furnish this with more specificness, the November in this case being that located in the year of 2016. It was prior to this temporal enclosure that a quantity of events had occurred regarding possesionality of the McLaren organisation and a significant integer of these events had not proceeded in a manner that would bring to me an emotion in the spectrum of pleased. Nonetheless, it was a quantity of importantness to myself that I maintained a continuity of professionalityness, especially towards my fellow holders of shares, e.g. Mansour Ojjeh.

However, it was with some unfortunateness that Mr Ojjeh visited the operational zone referred to in some instances as 'my office', during the time period aforesaid as being that of a November, and specifically in 2016. A conversation was commenced which was of a frank yet cordial nature, during which a human assistance unit, sometimes referred to as 'my PA' brought for Mr Ojjeh a quantity of liquid, being of a high temperature nature and contained in a handled vessel, this being what should be henceforth considered as 'a mug of tea'. This vessel was held by Mr Ojjeh in the leftmost of his two hands, permitting the low-flow consumption of the beverage in a manner that met with all the parameters of cautiousness until sensors mounted in Mr Ojjeh's lips and/or mouth could return some useable data regarding liquid temperature. This being then established as outside of the normal operating window considered optimal for human consumption, Mr Ojjeh enacted a placing movement to temporarily divest himself of the need to maintain contact with the vessel by manoeuvrising it over and then downwards upon a horizontal plane of more than adequate surface area, this being the object known as 'my desk'. It is with no small unfortunateness, that Mr Ojjeh's placement chose to ignore the reasonable parameters for high temperature vessel containment strategies, being as it was upon the deskal surface directly, despite the visible provision of an optimally sized disk of a heat resistant nature, that being an item in the known spectrum of 'a coaster'.

Upon regarding this sub-optimal placement I rapidly experienced a high quantity of a human emotion within the spectrum of rage. This internal experience was then rapidly conveyed to Mr Ojjeh utilising data communication channels of an aural and physical sub-set.

Within a low quantity of days, Mr Ojjeh and his cohorts had downloaded to myself through printed media of an A4 nature, transported within a paper capsule of a smaller area, that I was to be directed towards an area of the Paragon facility of a type that is marked with the word 'exit'. It is resultant from this circumstancitutde explained forthwith that I am now seeking a quantity of allowance that is in the spectrum of that for jobseekers.

I hope this communication has provided the quantity of clarity for which you were expectant. Transmission ends.

# TEAM PROFILE - RENAULT

**Full name:** Renault Sport Formula One Team
**Car:** R.S.17
**Engine:** Renault
**Drivers:** Nico Hulkenburg, Jolyon Palmer

The team that used to be one of the Lotuses is back for its second season as Renault with a new strategy, which is to give its drivers overalls that inexplicably make them look like camp trawlermen. Also, they've had another crack at the engine and promise that it'll be better this year, if only so they can optimise the packaging in order to shove it up Christian Horner's arse. Cyril Abiteboul is somehow in control or at least maintaining that illusion whilst simultaneously retaining his position as member of the paddock who most resembles that French skiing instructor your wife fancies even though she 'doesn't normally go for bald men'. Meanwhile, Jolyon Palmer keeps his seat in the car and will be sure to turn in another world class performance in the specific areas of having a head that looks too old for the rest of him and saying the word 'guys' on the radio in really needy way. Ken Magnussen moves out of the other car, leaving the way open for Nico Hulkenburg, a man so dependable he sometimes returns his neighbour's lawnmower in better condition than when he borrowed it. Disappointingly, however, the driver often known by his obvious nickname of 'The Nburg' will not be attempting another combined F1/Le Mans driving offensive, perhaps due to as-yet-undisclosed plans to star in the entire seasons of both BTCC and CSI: Dusseldorf.

# TRACK GUIDE - USA

**Track:** Circuit of the Americas
**Race date:** 22 October

One of the current calendar's purpose-built tracks, Circuit of the Americas was designed by Tilke Engineering but Hermann must have been out that day because they've accidentally left in some overtaking opportunities and it's all quite interesting. With its mixture of fast and slow corners, this track is a real challenge for car and driver, whilst the challenge for viewers at home is to get through all the TV coverage of commentators and pundits hinting at what a good time they're having in Austin without throwing a vase at the television. Ultimately, this is a track that presents the audience with many questions: Who will get a good run up the hill from the start and lead into the tight first corner? Who has got the best set-up compromise to tackle the range of corners? And, most importantly, how do you get invited up into that tower thing? It never looks like there's that many people up there. Is it ticketed? Do you have to know someone? Is it not actually that good once you're up there and everyone just leaves again?

## UNITED STATES OF AMERIC-O-FACTS
- Due to an uncorrected error dating back to 1959, the average American is advised to eat 90 pounds of butter per week.
- The United States has two official national anthems. One is 'The Star-Spangled Banner'. The other is, 'shirtless man repeatedly shouting USA! USA! out of the window of a moving pick-up truck'.
- Due to a scheduling error, the US political system has accidentally been replaced with an episode of hit NBC sit-com, 'Doll Handed Piss Licker Goes To Washington'.

# TRACK GUIDE - MEXICO

**Track:** Autódromo Hermanos Rodríguez
**Race date:** 29 October

After the successful return of the Mexican Grand Prix in 2015, F1 is back at the venue that literally translates as 'the Rogers Brothers Racetrack'. This is a very different circuit from the last time F1 was here, or indeed the time before that. In particular, the once-banked Peraltada was deemed far too interesting for modern F1 and has been replaced by some slow corners and a drive through the venue for an entirely different sport. Nonetheless, this is a fast track and one that can be tough on drivers thanks to the altitude, which can make it difficult to say 'the guys did a great job' without getting breathless. There's another challenge for the top three drivers because the podium is bloody miles from the motorhome and it's a long trek back when you're covered in Champagne or, in the case of Kimi Raikkonen, full of it. On the plus side, an enthusiastic crowd are certain to go wild for local boy Sergio Perez, and also for Lewis Hamilton, assuming that by October he'll have probably adopted a Mexican accent.

## MEXIC-O-FACTS
- Mexico is a founding member of MATA, a pan-global trade body made up of countries where the moustache is still acceptable.
- Mexico City is so densely populated that it's said all tap water has been through at least four people, as indeed has all food.
- The best way to make a Mexican laugh is to tell them they'll have to pay for a wall.

# TEAM PROFILE - SAUBER

**Full name:** Sauber F1 Team
**Car:** C36
**Engine:** Ferrari
**Drivers:** Marcus Ericsson, Pascal Wehrlein

Sauber's traditional position as the thinking fan's midfield team has been undermined in recent seasons, largely by their inability to get into the midfield. Now denied the embarrassment damper of Manor behind them, the Swiss team has to try a new tack which is either to invite 10 new and useless extra teams to drive around behind them, or to get better. They seem to have opted for the latter strategy, starting with binning that crap livery that made them look like a low-level GP2 team and replacing it with a smart, elegant paint scheme that is refreshingly untainted by sponsors. Team boss Monisha Kaltenborn will need to do something about that in order to make the most of their Ferrari power, assuming of course she hasn't accidentally signed a contract stipulating that in fact their engines must be supplied by Giedo van der Garde. Driver-wise, the team has a mixed bag on its hands with computer generated race child Pascal Wehrlein showing great promise before he was shunted by an elderly Brazilian man at the Race of Champions while Marcus 'Sony' Ericsson has been in the sport so long that everyone has pretty much realised he's not very good and is employed largely because he's punctual and has nice hair.

# TRACK GUIDE - BRAZIL

**Track:** Autódromo José Carlos Pace
**Race date:** 12 November

The Interlagos track is one of the most demanding and exciting on the calendar, especially for TV music researchers who must spend hours finding those tracks that have all the drums on them and that funny instrument that sounds a bit like a squeaky insect. The circuit itself presents a heady combination of fast and slow corners, elevation changes, and the possibility that a load of piss will leak all over the track like it did that time a few years ago. Also, sometimes the weather is cack. Drivers like coming here because the crowds are so enthusiastic and things will be especially emotional for local boy Felipe Massa, mainly because he'll have to hand back all the retirement presents people gave him last year.

## BRAZIL-O-FACTS
- Brazil hosted the 2016 Olympics, the 2014 World Cup and every round of the global championships for jiggling about in a really arse cracky bikini.
- The capital of Brazil is Brasilia even though everyone thinks it's not.
- Football is hugely popular in Brazil and the national team are very successful, mostly because they're really good at football.
- Brazil gives its name to both a type of nut and a type of Alan.

# TRACK GUIDE - ABU DHABI

**Track:** Yas Marina Circuit
**Race date:** 26 November

After the excitement and colour of Brazil, the F1 season comes to its new close with the dusty fart of the Abu Dhabi race. Literally no one's favourite track, Abu Dhabi is popular only amongst people who like races that go dark halfway through and fans of pit exits that look like you're trying to escape from a Sainsbury's car park near Shrewsbury. Such is drivers' disdain for the circuit described as 'sort of like Bahrain but with a light up hotel' that Kimi Raikkonen once openly described it as 'shit', although that might have been because he was struggling to find anywhere that served booze.

## ABU DHAB-O-FHACTS
- The Yas Marina area is dominated by the distinctive Ferrari World building, although around the corner there is also a Lamborghini World which is brighter and noisier and has more interesting doors.
- Abu Dhabi literally translates as 'even more boring Dubai'.
- Abu Dhabi is the largest of the United Arab Emirates, and also has the most golden things.

## CRAZY DAVE COULTHARD

**The former driver looks back on those from the class of 2016 who won't be with us this season**

Och aye tha noo muthafuckas. Crazy Dave Coulthard comin' atcha on tha Chazzel Fouzzle. Cuz showin' all races live is fo' losers.

So we is about to start the Fiddy Uno season for oh-seventeezle but befo' we all be like chattin' about tha shizzle fo' tha new season, Crazy D gonna ask yo to pour one out for ma fallen homies who kept it real in twenty sizzleteen but ain't comin' back fo' mo'. Cuz that be tha truth about Fo' 1. One minute you cock o' tha tight trousahs, next you is wondering why Sebastian Vettel is parked in yo space at tha Red Bull crib. Enforced retirementizzle.

So, laydeez and homies, let's take a moment of silence fo' tha dearly departed, starting with my brother E Gutizzy. Man, that Mexico muthafunker might o' looked like a sporty lesbian and once flipped ma buddy Nando like a pancake, but he gave it he's best shot. Save yo' tears, bredren, he be in a better place now. Formulizzle E-izzle.

We also sayin' peace-out to my so solid bro Filly Nas. Man, that dude ain't got enough letters in he's surname, but he sure tried hard in that shitty Saubizzle. In tha end, tha homie got taken down by tha cruellest cut of all. Inadequatizzle development budgetizzle.

An' now we get to tha big dogs. Crazy D be feelin' a little emosh here crew, cuz we sayin' goodbye to my so solid weird ear brother N Rosbiddy. Man, that dude got every ting a F1 homie be wishin' fo'. Sweet ride, Wo' Championshizzle, an' a team mate he really like beatin' cuz he hate him. Fo' sho'. An' he jus' walk away. Pure mental, innit. Peace out homie, you got some ting else now. Spendizzle more time with yo' familizzle.

I'm wellin' up now, homedogs, cuz lastly we get to a difficult one for Tha D to speak about. My brother from a West Country mutha, ma so solid bro, my croaky voice homie Jenny B. You at peace now, cuz. You no longer sufferin'. You don't have to drive that shitizzle MacdaddyLaren and be havin' dem conversations wit' Nanny O about how hey, wouldn't it be faster to, like, walk the track. It all over. But hey, you should get wit' tha programme man. Tha C4 TV programme. If you like, Crazy D even lend you a pair of tighty whitey trousahs. Lucratizzle punditrizzle positionizzle.

Peace and love brothers and lady brothers. Crazy D out. But please do join me on Channel 4 on Sunday 26 March for a full package of highlights as we look at all the on-track action from the season opening race in Australia.

Thanks to Ben Lucareli, Andrew Perry,
Jules, Dylan and bump.

This is the end of the Sniff Petrol 2017 Grand Prix Guide.
Please now turn off the book and allow it to cool down.

Printed in Great Britain
by Amazon